How To Leave ⌐ully

A step by step guide to leaving an abusive relationship
and making a new start

To Nikki
with best wishes for
Kate
XX

YouCaxton Publications

24 High Street, Bishop's Castle, Shropshire. SY3 8JX
www.youCaxton.co.uk

Published in Great Britain by
Katie Waistell

ISBN 978-1-90644-05-2

Cover Illustration © Katie Waistell

Photo on Reverse © Sue Reeves www.suepix.co.uk

Printed and bound in Great Britain.

How To Leave a Bully

A step by step guide to leaving an abusive relationship
and making a new start

Katie Waistell

There are writers and philosophers who will say it is the freedom of the mind that is the most valuable thing in life. How dreadful it is then when it's your closest relationship which threatens this - not a prison; not an interrogator; not a political regime but your partner.

There have been many studies around the state of 'happiness'.

Neuro-scientist Dr Lynda Shaw observes that "When the brain is in a pleasurable state we are more effective, healthier and productive. However the ever-increasing demands of modern life can interrupt previously established norms and expectations, perpetuating low self-esteem, poor communication, fear of failure and isolation. Not only is this devastating on a personal level, but destructive and corrosive within a work environment" This may ring true to you if you are in an unhappy relationship. We simply function better if we are happy.

Contents

INTRODUCTION

If you're feeling your relationship with your partner has reached a point of no return but are unsure (and scared stiff!) of the next step, this might be the book for you. However I would stress it certainly hasn't been written as a destructive force – a marriage or relationship breaker - but rather as a constructive element in your decision-making, helping you review where you are now and where you want to be in the future.

You may be in a long term relationship where it feels as though your lives - children; mortgage; job; friends are so entwined it's impossible to imagine untwining them – and then, once untwined, you'd need to look at making a whole new life for yourself – staying put may seem the only option. Eleven years ago, I was where you are now. I too looked at a tangled mess and couldn't think where to begin. But begin I did and I hope my experience will contribute something to yours.

I've split the process I followed, into three clear and different stages. I feel these stages are actually emotional or 'mind set steps' and whilst there are a number of them to take during the process, you'll do them in the order which best suits you – there's no right or wrong way of doing things, just *your* way. Practicalities and mindset will help you follow your own path, your own three steps.

Before going into the details of those steps, I wanted to talk a bit about relationship breakdowns and their causes. I've focused on abusive relationships because this is what I have directly experienced. I haven't written this book as a trained counselor, lawyer or psychiatrist, just a woman who's learned from her own experiences and would like to pass those on. The views expressed are mine alone but where I've felt a more authoritative or qualified source is required, I've listed further reading and pointed you in the right direction to find it. It is my sincere hope that as you read, you'll take comfort in knowing you're not alone in your situation.

There are, of course, many books which offer a practical guide to getting a divorce. But the majority of these seem pretty mechanical – they tell you what to *do* but not how you might *feel*. They don't address the emotional impact of that major initial decision to split. Nor do they address the anxieties chasing around in your head, not least of which is - *what about life afterwards?*

There are also any number of self-help books, life coaches and personal development coaches out there. But the fact was that when I was trapped in my abusive relationship I felt completely alienated from all this activity and information. Magazine articles were irrelevant; courses were inaccessible; self help was superficial. The deep stomach churning level of fundamental unhappiness I was experiencing blocked any ability to engage in this sort of 'tweaking' at the edges advice and assistance. I needed to go through something far more life changing, risky and scary before looking at myself and assessing what I wanted from life; what I wanted to achieve and whether I wanted to feng shui my bathroom!

It's an undeniable fact when considering leaving a relationship that there are innumerable practical issues to be considered which listed, can seem insurmountable. So insurmountable in fact that you might feel you should remain exactly where you are – unhappy, probably lonely and living with someone who, for a variety of reasons you really don't want to be with. I hope some of what I have to say will be helpful.

NB: Although throughout the book I refer to matters concerning children in the context of your relationship I hope the principles of my ramblings are helpful even if you don't have children to consider in your 'move'.

MY OWN STORY

Throughout the book I've included contributions from other women who have experienced a similar situation but for starters here's a bit of my story...

I met my husband when I was 22; I was quite an insecure 22 year old and financially hard up. I worked and socialised with people more affluent than myself and wanted a part of that world. My husband was 15 years older than me. I was impressed with his seemingly sophisticated lifestyle and his attention was flattering.

We started dating and his behaviour moved very swiftly to that of a bully and looking back I'm still astonished at how quickly I became trapped. At this stage, of course, I could have walked away and the number of times I look back with regret, are countless.

Our relationship was flawed from the start but I stayed with it. I wanted to show him he needn't feel insecure about me and that his jealous rages were unnecessary. I tried to reassure him I was in the relationship for the long term.

Now I can look back and clearly see, because I was insecure I assumed he must be too. I therefore offered all the reassurances that in fact I needed from a relationship.

I chose to get pregnant and felt excited and confident that things would change and we'd have a smoother future. Of course this never happened and the relationship became a long, dark tunnel of emotional abuse - until the day I left ...

When I did, my life became my own again; I was my own person and ever since I've been living on the fantastic fresh air that freedom brings.

I should say and this is perhaps most important of all - I have two wonderful daughters by my ex-husband who bring me continuous happiness and of whom I'm so very proud. I have not a single regret about having my daughters but I do regret he was their father. What might our lives have been like if they had been born into a happy family?

My ex-husband died at the beginning of 2012, eleven years after I left him. With his death came a huge and unexpected wave of emotions I couldn't identify or control. It was as though a damn had burst, spewing out an unimaginable amount of grief, anger and sadness.

If it weren't for the death of my ex-husband I think I might not have revisited my emotions in this way. But I did and it's prompted me to write this book with the hope it may provide another woman with the torch she needs to light her way out of the tunnel.

I spent eleven years with him and now eleven years have passed since I left him. So I've had as much time away from the abuse as I had taking it. In these last years my life has been fabulous and simpler - I'm free to make decisions about myself, my family, my girls and I have a very lovely husband who shows none of the traits of my ex-husband. I feel incredibly grateful. I also have a lovely boy, a wonderful addition to my family.

So in the most positive way I would like to empower you (and whilst I've been talking about women, men can suffer equally in an abusive relationship.) to find a way out, start over and give yourselves the chance of a simpler, fabulous life – you deserve it as much as I did.

ACKNOWLEDGING THE PROBLEM

HAVE YOU REACHED THE POINT OF NO RETURN?

A **long-term relationship in which love, time and resources have been invested deserves respect. A decision to move on should never be taken lightly, particularly where children are involved. In most societies, it's accepted that relationships provide security; status; credibility and often offspring. It is also accepted that the most successful relationships are those where goals are shared.**

At the opposite end of the spectrum are relationships that hit a brick wall. Of course, nothing is ever black and white and sometimes there are combinations of issues. Your current difficulties may be caused by abusive behavior, affairs or simply growing apart. I have focused on abusive behaviour but you may also find the book useful if the other categories apply.

CAN WE FIX IT? There are some issues that can be fixed, relationships worked on, revived or rescued. Others cannot be put right and the only solution to protect yourself and your children, if you have them, is to LEAVE.

IF IT'S NOT FIXABLE, CAN IT BE LIVED WITH? Many couples with differences in attitude and behaviour find a way of getting along, respecting their partner's views and allowing each other the space to live a fulfilling life. Reasons for this may be children; extended family; time already invested in the relationship; mutual friends; housing; employment and so on. These couples may not have a perfect relationship but they find a way to make things work.

However, a destructive relationship can gnaw away at your very core leaving you a shell of your former self. People I speak to in such situations all use similar language – *"Not being true to myself"; "Functioning like a robot"; "Programmed to think in an unnatural way"*. The other thing they all share is that they all tried to convince themselves the problems would go away. All hoped that as their partner developed trust, jealousy and bullying would become a thing of the past. Sadly they also all found this not to be the case.

> MARIE: When I was with my husband I felt like a flower wilting in a cupboard, everything was dark and I just couldn't grow or be the flower I was meant to be. Since leaving him I have started to grow and feel more myself but I've also accepted some of the responsibility for what happened and this has made me feel empowered, I feel I can now change my future and feel less of a victim.

Never forget the effects of a destructive relationship are insidious. A frog which leaps into a pan of boiling water will immediately leap back out. A frog which leaps into a pan of cold water will happily swim around as the pan heats up. The frog doesn't notice boiling point is being reached until it's too late! A painful but true analogy!

ABUSIVE BEHAVIOUR

Whether verbal or physical, abuse has a devastating effect. It destroys your sense of self. You begin to lose your identity and the happiness of being you along with all your self-confidence and creativity. It strangles exploration and enjoyment of new activities and ideas. It stifles self-expression and stops you thinking freely.

When I was with my abusive husband I sought counseling, I loved him and wanted to save my marriage but needed coping skills. The question was, could I change his abusive behavior?

I never imagined leaving my husband but, worryingly often thought about killing him! It seemed a more achievable option! Of course my practical side stopped short of smothering him with a pillow when he was in a drunken stupor - good thing because I 'd now be in prison and the girls would have had no parents at all!

The counseling had an amazing impact on my ability to cope although it took ten sessions to build up techniques I could use to protect myself. My counselor was highly trained and probably knew that as my inner strength grew I would come to the point of realizing the abuse was **UNACCEPTABLE**.

Because my confidence was shot to pieces and my mind so jumbled, re-building my self-confidence was incredibly hard. I found coherent thought, when I wasn't at work, almost impossible. Consequently when I was working, thinking straight was an enormous and exhausting effort.

I used affirmations (almost impossible at first, I couldn't say the words in my head, let alone out loud.) My councilor suggested I start by writing them down. My affirmations were:

"I am a good mother."
"I am a good wife."
"I am kind and considerate."
"I am loyal."
"I am capable and organized."

In addition to the affirmations, I was advised to break the habit of the abuse by removing myself physically from the room. When my husband started an argument, I was taught to say "I'm not having this conversation, I can see where it's going." and remove myself from the room. Sometimes it worked, sometimes it didn't. But when it did, the power balance in the relationship began to shift.

In retrospect I think it was with this shift that his depressive bouts and more severe drinking really kicked in. He became introverted and full of self-pity. He either wouldn't go to work or if he did would come home at lunchtime. By the time I got back from work he would be drunk; he wouldn't see friends and certainly didn't want me to.

But, as I fought for my self-confidence, gradually the clutter cleared from my mind and one day like a blinding light I realised that I could just go with my children and set up a new life without him.

The website Refuge advises the following on recognizing abuse:

Emotional abuse: "*Many women experience domestic violence without ever being physically abused. Sometimes they're not sure if what is happening to them is domestic violence. They worry that no-one will take them seriously if they talk about it.*

If you alter your behaviour because you are frightened of how your partner will react, you are being abused. Emotional abuse is an attack on your personality rather than your body.

Emotional abuse can be just as harmful as physical abuse. It often leads to physical violence over time."

MARIE: My husband starved me of physical affection. He never kissed or hugged me. In fact he never touched me apart from when we had sex (which was a thoroughly mechanical process). The last kiss he ever gave me was on our wedding day which was about seven years before I left him. He criticised my body after I had children. It took me years to find the confidence to take my clothes off in front of anyone else again.

THE EFFECTS OF AN ABUSIVE RELATIONSHIP

The effects of an ongoing abusive relationship can be varied and extremely long-reaching:

- Long term bullying eventually leaves the recipient unsure of who they are; totally lacking in self-confidence; unpredictably emotional; irrational and experiencing states of elation followed by deep depression.

- You can suffer depression with a sense of low or no self-worth; be unable to connect to day-to-day life; feel unable to make basic decisions and be unwilling to engage in other personal relationships with family and friends.

- Basic day-to-day activities may become overwhelming, for example: attending a PTA meeting; helping your child with homework or simply collecting items from the dry cleaners, all of these may become exhausting and difficult.

- As the situation worsens - your memory plays tricks and you forget things your partner has brought to your attention as being important. Your unhappy subconscious seems to work against you. You day-dream while cooking dinner and burn it; you forget to get dinner out of the freezer; you go into the shop to buy bread and beer and come out with milk.

All of the above may sound trivial but if you are recognizing it and are saying "That's me!", rest assured it was me too

It is truly terrifying to be aware that your individuality; personality; identity and life blood are being leached, leaving you quite literally an empty shell. It's scary to know that each day, month, year that passes you are becoming less of your true self. Insomnia, night sweats; voices in your head; irrational behaviour; shouting at colleagues; crying in front of your neighbours and your children; extreme mood swings, all are symptomatic of being eaten away from inside.

LIVING WITH BULLYING: In a relationship where the fundamentals are flawed you learn that to express a strong opinion leads to further misery – the mysterious loss of sentimental and precious items such as a recipe written out by your grandma; interrogation over why you like a certain TV presenter – "Do you fancy him?" "Do you wish you were with him not me?" Or it may be the loss of a favorite piece of clothing; CDs; never being able to visit a favorite holiday destination or even a shop just because you said you liked them. Having things you like withdrawn is a method of control and an infliction of misery.

Over time, many things become a secret kept to yourself as you learn to hide your thoughts and feelings. It can even become a bit of game. A record comes on the radio – you show no visible signs of liking or disliking but inside you might be dancing or reliving a certain experience. A part of your mind is still free to feel and experience something hidden from your partner.

Bizarre as it sounds you may even say you don't like something just to protect it – the teapot your mother gave you – that means it'll stay; you don't like U2 or Cold Play – so you can listen to them in the future.

Do you recognize the above? Can you see yourself in the picture I've painted? You're not alone, there are so many people I've had the privilege to tell my story to and they in turn have opened up and told me how trapped they felt when they were with their partner – or sadly still feel because they don't know how to leave.

When you've been brought low by bullying it can be so very hard to find the motivation; the energy; the clarity of thought to change your life. I hope that this book helps: firstly by helping you recognise the situation; secondly reassuring you that you are NOT alone and thirdly showing you the steps you can take. You can break free and rediscover who you are; regain your mind and find yourself once more.

Bullying often starts quite mildly – a few put downs; criticism over a decision you've made; undermining you in front of your friends, telling you what you can and can't wear. All of which demands an unreasonable level of your time and attention.

I remember visiting my mother on mother's day in the first month of my relationship; my bullying man was in hospital (he'd admitted himself saying he was having a heart attack when he clearly wasn't - more of that later!). When I got back from my mother's he was outraged and for the remaining eleven years of our relationship he would bring this up again and again, reminding me how I'd put my mother first over him when he was ill in hospital. Of course I regretted going to my mum's but we'd only been dating for four weeks and were not even that close at that stage!

A bully craves attention – they want all of your time. They're threatened by others who take your time, even their own children.

When my 2 girls were born in each case I didn't have eye contact with my husband for about 6 weeks after the birth. I felt helpless to do anything about it - the baby needed my attention and was certainly going to get it. But his behaviour affected how I cared for my children thereafter. The babies were not allowed in our room at night. If they woke I had to ensure they didn't come in our bedroom. My husband's sleep must never be disturbed or I would be accused of putting the children before him. Since having my youngest child, twelve years later and by a different father, I now realise how bizarre this behaviour was, but at the time I accepted it - I wanted to make things right.

Bullies feel threatened by any close relationships you may have. For example, my ex-husband prevented me communicating with my best friend for about six years, destroying letters from her and ensuring I had no way of making contact. Bullies may even be threatened by unreachable people such as celebrities, in fact anyone in whom you take an interest.

A bully's mood can change at an alarming rate. Being on the receiving end of this is horrible. You see that dark threatening look, that shadow and think "Oh God, here we go". You wrack your brains trying to think what you've done to cause this and just pray the spell won't last long. You contemplate events happening in the next week or so which might be ruined by this latest mood swing.

Your legs turn to jelly and your stomach flips, you feel sick and your mouth fills with a gush of saliva. Your body reacts physically to the very real fear of how the mood will progress.

Bullies are incredibly deceitful – they ensure no-one else can see what's going on inside the relationship. They will often go out of their way to give the impression they care about you more than anyone in the world and would do anything for you. But behind closed doors things are very different.

It's hard, because you want to cry for help. You want others to see what's going on and sometimes you explode. This inevitably backfires with people either assuming you're stressed and overreacting to something minor or that you're slightly unhinged – all of which makes them sympathise with your husband.

When I look back at photos (not something I do very often, I find it emotionally draining, but I recently put together some photos for my girls birthdays - 21 and 18 this year) nearly every photo brings back a memory of some terrible row; not being spoken to for a week; being berated for something I'd said. On some of the photos I look very pale and thin. It's too scary to think that I could have stayed that way.

I'd be having a lovely day out and then in the course of a normal conversation mention a place or someone's name and that would be it -the awful bullying session would start and typically last about 3 days.

A bully will twist words; keeping on and on until you can't think straight and certainly feel you can't do anything right. A bully can at times seem incredibly kind, a few gentle gestures and you think "He does love me" Looking back I don't know what he was thinking when he was in this mode. Was he being normal or was he simply buying my attention?

My counselor recommended I read up on transactional analysis. This is where one person behaves as 'parent' and the other as 'child' instead of 'adult to adult'. I fell into this trap and when the bullying kicked in would revert to 'child' mode. This behaviour became a pattern and its familiarity provided a strange sort of comfort.

In reading about transactional analysis I immediately recognised that behaviour in myself and hard though it was, took steps to correct it. I found a way to have more equality in my relationship - though it was a short lived period prior to me leaving.

A bullying partner will often see and set themselves up as an authority on good parenting. This provides a platform from which to undermine a partner in any number of different settings – in front of children, relatives, even the school. It is a very effective form of control.

Is this you? Are you in a situation where your partner considers himself to be the authority on parenting, even if he's not particularly a 'hands on' parent? My ex-partner didn't do bath time, never read to the children but rather saw himself as the critical observer – he certainly believed he had the right to dominate parenting and be the decision maker. When your partner is doing this, no matter how good a mother/father you are, you can be made to feel not good enough and that you need to be taught how to parent.

Any arrogant assumption about parenting ability often comes with a complete lack of understanding of what being a parent is all about and this is reflected in the lack of attention that in reality is given to the children. Remind yourself now – you have the SAME and EQUAL rights as your partner. The fact they may be the main bread winner does NOT make them superior to you. It DOES NOT mean they can teach you right, wrong and above all it does not mean that they know how to be a good parent.

WHERE DOES BULLYING BEHAVIOR COME FROM? Statistics show it is men who are more likely to be the bully in a relationship and so for this reason this book may speak more to women. But the same principles apply - if you're being bullied by your partner it's not acceptable and it's NOT YOUR FAULT. Bullying in a relationship is unacceptable whether physical or as is often more frequently the case, emotional.

Bullies have often themselves been bullied. They may have been badly treated when they were younger by parents, siblings, school friends; teachers. They may have been or are being bullied at work. They can transfer all this to their partner at home. But *background* does *not* excuse *bullying*. When you are the victim of a bully it is highly likely you blame yourself for your partner's behaviour. Initially, love for your partner will make you look for ways to change your own behaviour to prevent the bullying.

You will make excuses, turning the situation around to blame yourself. Was it what you wore that day? Did you spend too long on the phone? Had you focused too much attention on the children and not enough on your partner? Had you overspent on food this week? When you're in a bully's clutches you very swiftly lose your sense of perspective.

A bully is consciously manipulative. They look for excuses to exert control and in truth, nothing will change that. Bullies only change if they choose to and in my experience this is unlikely. Trying to improve your relationship by discussing the matter with your bullying partner can be one of the scariest options and in fact often totally impossible. It can also lead to more severe bullying, threats, extreme behaviour and punishment.

IS INEQUALITY IN YOUR RELATIONSHIP DRIVING THE BULLYING? The root cause of bullying is a fundamental (and fatal) combination of inequality and insecurity whether real or perceived. However root causes are not excuses! Inequality may spring from differences in education; salary; relationship with family; age; self-confidence or intellectual ability. All or any of these can cause insecurity and in so many instances, insecurity is a self-fulfilling emotion.

TO ILLUSTRATE: An individual will come across something in the course of their daily life that destabilises their already damaged sense of security. Instead of shaking off that feeling, they look for confirmation that it's genuine. It's then not hard to find any number of endorsements and as the grievance grows it festers until it erupts in anger, interrogation and argument. This sequence is often repeated over a set time span. You may wonder why you seem to argue every three months. Why your partner throws a wobbly on a Saturday morning or every time you visit a certain place. It's because the behaviour has become a habit which is comforting in itself.

The arguing has become a game in which you are both players. Engage in the argument; retaliate in the same way each time and you are feeding the pattern of behaviour. If you step outside the pattern and refuse to play the game you will cause a fundamental shift in your partner's behaviour pattern. You can refuse to engage; walk away. Use words like "Sorry I'm just not going down this path again".

You'll be amazed at how quickly this diffuses the situation but more importantly puts you back in control. The *game* often provides comfort and a form of security to both partners – a blazing row followed by extreme tears and sadness followed by dramatic making up; great sex; presents; comforting words. All of this can become habit forming. But it's unhealthy and I believe can take someone close to a nervous breakdown. One moment ecstatic happiness, contentment and euphoria, the next at your wits end and in a pit of self-pity and despair.

WHERE IS YOUR RELATIONSHIP NOW?

All relationships have their ups and downs or hit rocky patches and sometimes we have to dig deep to make things work. But there are usually very strong reasons why you're together in the first place and the rewards for 'working at it' can often be far greater than you might have imagined. You may end up with a stronger, more stable and infinitely more precious relationship than before. Sometimes though, there are issues that are unresolvable.

The National Family Mediation web site offers the following advice regarding divorce:

"To be ready for divorce is to have a lower emotional attachment to the person you are separating from, otherwise, the divorce process itself will be roller coaster of intense feelings, including anger, distrust and hurt. A statement that would indicate that you are making a sincere, rather than an emotionally reactive decision is, 'I acknowledge that you are a person in your own right with your own personality, hopes and dreams, I can respect you for that, but I no longer want to be married to you.'"

YOU'RE MENTALLY READY TO LEAVE, SO HOW DO YOU MAKE IT HAPPEN? You can see your relationship has no future *BUT* doing something about it seems impossible.

Why is this? One answer is fear and fear has a lot to answer for! It's the reason for your trapped feelings; the reason the relationship has become so unbalanced; it's why you're putting up with your own bizarre behavior. Additionally you may be feeling:

- Fear of being alone

- Fear of being intimidated

- Fear of being shouted at

- Fear of being belittled

- Fear of being made to feel inadequate

- Fear of losing even more contact with friends; family; children

- Fear of losing your partner who at one time you loved with all your heart

- Fear of losing financial stability

- Fear of losing contact with your children

- Fear of losing credibility and status among friends

If there was nothing to fear what would you do? Of course I understand your fear is very real as is your fear of further abusive behaviour. This threat is real and you need to protect yourself and your children if you're going to take the step to leave.

ANOTHER REASON FOR BEING STUCK is perhaps your perceived inability to change the situation? Sadly the fact you've been made weaker over time leads to more resistance to changing the situation. Remember our frog in the pot analogy? What's happened to you has been insidious, over a period of time you've learned to accept abnormal behavior - not just from your partner but also from yourself. There are many compelling reasons to maintain the status quo and as day follows day you just go with the flow. The situation you're in is dysfunctional but for you has it begun to feel normal.

YOU NEED A KICK START – GRAB A PEN AND PAPER . . .

- Write a list of adjectives to describe yourself as you are now.

- And again to describe how you'd want to be in the future.

- How might your children, friends or family describe you now?

- What would you like them to be saying?

- Write a list of adjectives to describe your ideal partner. What would you like to see on the list? How mismatched is this from your current situation?.

BID FOR FREEDOM

Allow yourself to dream in detail, really visualise a better and happier future. Draw a picture if it helps – just a few doodles or sketches. Cut out pictures from magazines – keep them in a folder or if you're able, stick them on a board or in a scrap book. You may of course need to keep this hidden from your partner.

You should know you are actually free to choose your own path and take control. It just doesn't feel that way at the moment and it's probably impossible to imagine. But it's time to start making these thoughts a reality.

As yet you probably haven't discussed your level of unhappiness with your partner. You've probably tried to resolve differences but your partner is probably unaware you're now thinking of leaving. So the resistance to leave is coming from inside your *own head*. It's your fear which is making you think leaving can't be a reality.

SO WHAT WOULD YOU DO IF YOU COULD JUST GO?

- Where would you go?

- Who would you live with?

- Where would you live?

- Might your partner move out instead?

27

By addressing the above you will challenge the resistance in your mind and build confidence that your new future can be made reality. It will help you to feel confident and bold enough to strive for the freedom you deserve.

> *Marie: When I decided to leave my husband I planned the move and where I would go in quite a bit of detail. I committed to things such as the rental of a property so that no one would be able to talk me out of leaving. I knew I could easily carry on as things were but I had to leave for my own sanity. The more plans were fixed the more likely I was to carry them out. I was scared stiff.*

Marie also *worked* with her husband in the same company, part of her leaving plans were also getting another job. The day after she told her husband she was leaving she also handed in her notice. All parts of Marie's life were entwined and seemed to present insurmountable problems, but once she had made up her mind that was the route she was going to take Marie broke down the things that needed to be addressed and dealt with them one by one.

STEP 1
PLANNING

Continuing with the theme of making your dreams a reality the first consideration is the physical move and its timing. Timing may be key to the success of your plan. You need to consider big events that are coming up some as birthdays Christmas, weddings, family gatherings. Leaving when there is something like this coming up may make things much harder for you and may impact on the success of your plan, so look in the diary and check to see if there is a clear four week period ahead.

MOVING OUT VERSUS STAYING PUT? I believe if you want to be in control, you have to move out! Addressing the issue of your partner moving out of the marital/family home (if that is the right thing) can be dealt with later. You need to gain as much control as possible. You need to take the upper hand and be the one doing the moving. A solicitor may disagree as you might weaken your position legally. However, your solicitor is not living your life and doesn't know first-hand how difficult it is and how much easier things would be if you simply didn't live in the matrimonial home anymore. My advice is that if it feels right to get away, then take the risk.

Where are you going to move to? Can you move in with family or siblings? Can you move into a friend's house for a while? How much is rented accommodation in your area - is this feasible?

IF YOU HAVE CHILDREN then their needs will come first when considering where and how to move. Your options are:

- **MINIMUM UPHEAVAL** - ensuring they remain in the same school, can see their friends, see both parents; grandparents   etc

  OR the extreme opposite of this:

- **MOVING AWAY** completely even if it's just temporary. In this scenario you establish something new, to all of you. New school, new surroundings. This can have a positive effect as it can be exciting and a distraction. The downside to this for you, as an adult, can be harder as you may be more alone. You may also feel a sense of having run away and not being able to face up to the reality of the situation.

MY ADVICE REMAINS THE SAME - all of this takes time. You need to deal with the whole issue of leaving your partner one step at a time. The physical aspect of moving is incredibly daunting – so go easy on yourself. Give yourself a bit of escapism or maybe a break if possible. This will buy you time to consider your future.

CONFIDING IN OTHERS

Don't be afraid to tell people what's going on, you'd be amazed at how common the problem is and you'll probably find, amongst your friends, you're not the only one and you can pick up helpful advice

SARAH: I wasn't sure how people would judge me when I left my husband. The majority of my friends had no idea that my marriage was so unhappy and would have been shocked and probably disbelieving had I confided in them. Abuse is not something everyone wants to talk about, they find it uncomfortable even distasteful and my experience is that people often think you're exaggerating at best or at worst you're the one who's gone mad and are making it all up.

Your mutual friends may not want to be seen to take sides, some will say "They need to sort things out for themselves". Or "There's two sides to every story!". But by remaining neutral they're actually supporting the abuser. They don't need to confront the abuser but they should if they are truly being supportive. They should make it clear to the abuser that they don't like what they've heard, they find it unacceptable, that you have their support; and they will be there for you. This, of course, is not always the case.

SALLY: The abuse from my husband was all verbal. When I left him I felt I needed to explain to my friends and family; but their look said it all; I think they thought it was either my fault or I was making it up. I felt they needed me to justify why I'd left and that I'd obviously not put in enough effort. Couldn't I have given him another chance? How much had I tried? Had I told him I was going to leave?

If you've never been on the end of verbal abuse I think it's difficult for people to relate to it. They don't know how bad it can be.

My family sent my ex-husband birthday cards not long after I'd left him. I wanted to scream "Do I need bruises for you people to see the shit that man put me through?" I still can't rationalise why they supported him.

You need to be prepared to lose mutual friends. When I left my husband I didn't stay friends with anyone I had met through my marriage. They couldn't make the journey with me and I couldn't get bogged down with the effort required to keep the friendship going. However, the plus side was the close friends who pre-dated my marriage became even closer.

THE BEST CONFIDENTS are non-judgmental. They are in my experience people who've seen a fair amount of stress in their own lives; they've followed a rich and colourful path and don't have a black and white view. They may in fact not be your best friend or closest relative. Look around you - who might you be able to trust to just hold your hand through the early days of a split up?

YOU DON'T NEED TO JUSTIFY YOURSELF or tell every one of your friends and family how bad things have been. You don't need to lay your case bare for them to make judgment. It's often very hard for an abused person to speak of the abuse. It can often take years and sometimes will stay deeply buried forever. Those who support you don't require complete exposure from you. It's also a fact that an abuse victim will be blaming her/himself anyway, even without the help of a judgmental community; years of eroded self-confidence will make sure of that!

DON'T BE INFLUENCED by someone else's thoughts. It's essential that each decision is your own. It's good to run things past people and get their input but you don't want someone to engulf you and tell you what to do. Remember this is, after all, what you're trying to get away from.

> *Avoid Chat Rooms! They are time consuming; over emotional; sensational and can be poorly researched.*

GOOD FRIENDS and family members will help you make decisions around the children and come up with useful suggestions and assistance around housing in the early days. As before it's vital you stay in control, remember friends and family are there for support - not to tell you what to do - however they can be great when it comes to helping with the actual move!

PLANNING YOUR FINANCES

One of the most crucial and overwhelming considerations is where the hell you're going to live? Try to be easy on yourself - your first solution doesn't have to be the permanent solution. Ask family or friends for help you in the first few days or even weeks if that is the difference between making the initial step or staying put.

RENTED ACCOMMODATION:

Top tips:

- Research rents so you know what's a good deal.

- Don't leap at the first thing you see.

- Check out suitable areas for economic housing. I'd say living in the area you want is more important than a beautiful home, you can soon personalise it and in time may be able to decorate with the landlord paying for the paint etc. and you and your friends doing the DIY. So it may be cheaper or more economical to be nearer to the children's school or your place of work than in a nice pad the other end of town.

- Always negotiate on the rent.

- If necessary, borrow the deposit from friends/family or work.

- Make sure the rental contract includes a break clause – don't over-commit in the early days, not because you intend to go back but it's important to keep options open in terms of the future.

> *You may be eligible for housing benefit – check on line to see what might be available to you;*
> **www.gov.uk/housing-benefit/overview**
>
> *Also check your local council's website to see who you need to contact to apply for council housing.*
>
> *Emergency housing may also be an option. This is provided by charities such as Shelter or Women's Aid. You will find information on finding emergency housing for yourself and or your children on their websites.*

IT CAN BE DAUNTING STARTING AGAIN IN A NEW, UNFAMILIAR AND POSSIBLY SCRUFFY HOME. But you'll be amazed to find that once you have the ability to put your own personal touch on your home, you can be happy in almost any surroundings because you're free to move *your own* things around - something you may have been missing over the past few years! My sisters commented on the house I moved into with my children, exclaiming it actually looked like my house; possessions; ornaments; odds and ends they hadn't seen for years. It looked like my home because at last it was.

LIVING WITH PARENTS OR FRIENDS: This is a great short-term option and may be essential for the initial move. However pretty quickly you will need to communicate with them on your plans and manage their expectations.

AS A RULE OF THUMB if you've stayed at someone's house for 2 days - it will feel like 4 days to your host – particularly if you have children; so staying for a fortnight will feel like a month.

A month is long enough for anyone to host so my recommendation is to look at a 2 week stay with friends - max! Your parents may have more room and their perceptions of how long you've been there may be a little more realistic.

SOME TIPS FOR STAYING WITH FRIENDS:

- Set a timetable with a specified moving-out date.
- Try not to have an indefinite arrangement which puts pressure on both parties.
- No one means "You can stay as long as you like".
- Remember it's their house.
- Talk frequently and manage expectations of being guest/housemates
- Have fun!
- Have a plan and manage people's expectations.
    - When will you have found alternative accommodation?
    - When will you move there?

DOES FINANCE DRIVE THE ABOVE TIMESCALES? If finance is the issue can deadlines be brought forward to shorten the plan by throwing money at the problem? Can you ask your employers for a loan? Can you claim housing benefits? Can you ask your parents for a deposit? Some problems can be resolved by asking for help so don't be afraid to ask.

Budgeting – or how am I going to make the money last to the end of the month? My sister who's been a single parent of 3 strapping boys for the last 7 years seems to survive on nothing I asked her how she does it. Here are her top tips:

Food:

- Never put anything in your shopping basket unless you know the price.

- I shop with a basket not trolley.

- Buy only what you need and don't restock until you've run out.

- Never shop when hungry

- Plan your shopping; plan meals; involve the children in the planning. it may mean going to a few shops rather than the supermarket but for the children (depending on age) this can be fun.

House:

- Turn lights off. Reward your children for following the rules, fine them for lights left on.

- Turn the thermostat down and wear more clothes in winter.

- One-pot meals save on fuel.

- Try to use the oven for cooking only once or twice a week.

- Don't use a tumble dryer.

- *Make sure your rooms are as insulated as possible – draft excluders and lined curtains.*

- *There are plenty of cheap but good quality curtains at charity shops.*

- *Take meter readings so your bills are accurate and avoid any nasty catch up bills.*

- *Don't waste money on luxuries which have become the norm; Sky TV; takeaways; after-school clubs; gym membership; phones for every member of the family.*

- *Second hand things are OK. New things don't necessarily make you happy. Think about your life before you left – did material items make you happy? So don't feel pressured to buy new things – in fact enjoy the more relaxed lifestyle of living with things that are a bit careworn. Muddy shoes on the sofa won't be the crisis it once was.*

Clothing:

- *Don't buy any new clothes for about a year apart from cheap school uniforms for the children.*

- *After that, set yourself a strict budget and also see how long you can go without buying anything new.*

- *Buy secondhand clothes or do clothes swaps with friends.*

When I left my husband I had a good job and was financially secure but I still had to budget to ensure I could pay for birthdays, Christmas and holidays. My strategy was to be completely aware of the essential costs and what they were:

Rent or mortgage
Council tax (make sure you get the single adult discount)
Electricity
Gas
Food
Do not use credit cards - ever

WHEN LOOKING AT YOUR FINANCES don't forget to include your salary; child maintenance; child benefit and any other benefits to which you might be entitled.

> *To find out about benefits there are many helpful websites;*
> www.moneysavingexpert.com
> www.direct.gov.uk *(under money tax and benefits)*

CHILD MAINTENANCE: as a rule of thumb should be a minimum of 25% of your partner's take-home pay where you are providing the majority of the care. Family mediation services will be able to provide advice on what you can expect to receive.

> *You can find advice and links to local services at the National Family Mediation website:* www.nfm.org.uk.

You may not want to put yourself in a financial situation where you will be absolutely stuck without money from your ex because if this is the case it can provide an arena for them to regain control and manipulate your life once more.

If you have a job it's essential that this income is protected. Be straight with your boss/employer, tell them what's going on - this will probably buy you some time off but also a huge amount of support. Put your trust in people and you'll be surprised what they're prepared to give back. Don't be sensationalist - just honest – say what you need from your employers to support you through this rough patch.

OTHER OUTGOINGS AND EXPENSES TO TAKE INTO CONSIDERATION ARE:

TRANSPORT: Does moving mean you'll lose your source of transport? If so, make sure you move somewhere with good public transport. Can you get lifts for school and work? If so, what can you do in return for such help? Returning favours is an essential part of your new life - make sure you're in credit as much as possible. That way, in an emergency you can call on them.

TREATS: It's important to be straight with the children immediately - treats may have to go out the window for the moment. If the budget is zero then there are no treats for anyone. Children are realists and will soon stop asking for things. If you can afford it, budget for some treats but stick to that budget - don't overspend because of guilt.

UTILITIES: Utility bills can be scary so stay as informed as possible. Ask friends how much they spend. Shop around, make sure you're getting the best deal. Avoid housing with prepayment meters, as you'll be paying over the odds for gas and electricity. Economy Seven still exists, you'll know if you have this type of meter by looking at your electricity bill. Remember electricity at night is cheaper so run washing machines or dishwashers then.

CREDIT: this can be a slippery slope. If you have credit cards go to your bank and ask for their help in consolidating the debt and paying it off in affordable amounts. Do not take up any offer advertised on TV, online or in the paper as you will end up in a far worse situation.

PHONE BILLS: you only need one phone - if you have a mobile, ditch the house phone. Make sure you and the children are on pay-as-you go contracts and avoid phones that use the internet without you knowing, such as Blackberries. Use Sykpe or other similar free services as much as possible. Set targets for your monthly phone bill – go online and see where you are in terms of costs so far that month. The information is there - use it to your advantage.

FREEING UP YOUR TIME: Leaving a partner can free up an enormous amount of time - when you're not pandering to someone else's needs you'll be amazed at how much mental capacity and free space there is in your head not to mention spare time which you can use for supervising and helping with homework or taking the children on trips. In my first few weeks as a singleton we discovered the local library. It was such a simple but real treat to spend time choosing books for us all, and of course at no cost! At the library we also found out about other things going on in our area – often at no or low cost. You'll also find you have more time to see friends and family and have talking time which will be an enormous source of support.

LEGAL ADVICE

Good legal advice is essential and you should seek this is as soon as possible, ideally before you leave your partner. It may not affect what you decide to do but you'll be making a more informed and intelligent decision.

Don't be afraid of solicitors - In my experience they are not judgmental in any way but are in a position to provide good and impartial advice. They can also be quite sympathetic and directly supportive of you which will bolster your morale.

Legal aid: Solicitors are always going to be expensive so you need to check to see if you are eligible for legal aid. There's lots of information on the government's web site:

www.direct.gov.uk/en/governmentcitizensandrights/
gettinglegaladvice

TOP TIPS FOR SEEING A SOLICITOR:

- Try to see a solicitor who has been recommended, if not chose one who is conveniently located. You will probably need to see them a few times and a long journey or costly parking is an inconvenience you don't need.

- Always make notes, write down everything the solicitor says - you are paying for this advice and you need to make sure you have something to refer back to.

- All solicitors offer 30 minutes free consultation – this is where you can glean the most information about your current position - so write it down.

- Be prepared, take a list of questions, it doesn't matter how basic and silly you think they might be ask them anyway.

- Don't make assumptions based on what your friends think in terms of your legal position - check everything with the solicitor.

- A good solicitor will advise you on how you can keep your legal bill to a minimum. This will require you to do quite a bit of the work yourself.

- Ask for a regular statement (monthly) of costs incurred and your current balance.

- Remember you are in control of the process not the solicitor, you can move forward at your own pace.

- **YOUR SOLICITOR IS NOT YOUR FRIEND** – you don't need to chat on the phone about irrelevancies as this will only drive your costs up.

- Understand your current financial position as much as possible before approaching the solicitor: your mortgage costs, how many years left on the mortgage; your partner's earning, your earnings, other financial facts - loans; savings; joint insurance policies; any business arrangements there may be if either of you run your own business.

You need to write down this information so that you can have the most informative and constructive consultation as possible.

- It's also a good idea to keep a diary of conversations and activities after you have made the big move. Buy a hardback book and keep it somewhere safe. Make notes of telephone calls and conversations so you can keep a clear and balanced view of your partner's and your own behavior.

If they are making an unreasonable amount of calls, sending nasty text messages, bad-mouthing you; entering your property without invitation - keep a note of it as this sort of thing may be useful later should the legal process become difficult.

BECAUSE I'D MADE THE DECISION TO DIVORCE MY HUSBAND, it was the divorce which was my overriding priority.

I didn't want to be married to him any more and the finances, because I was in full time work, were less of a priority. I was in a weaker position in terms of the shared assets, the house wasn't in my name and my husband had lived there for twelve years prior to my arrival. But I was adamant I wanted to be divorced and less worried about the financial settlement. My solicitor was worried about doing it this way round and advised it might weaken my position further in terms of the finances but I knew that being divorced was essential to my mental and emotional confidence. So from start to finish my divorce took six months. The grounds were unreasonable behaviour and they were not contested.

The financial settlement came through twelve months later and because I was prepared to compromise on the level of child maintenance this was also relatively pretty quick

A good solicitor will urge cooperation between both of you in order to keep legal costs down. If you can discuss and agree a financial settlement without going through the courts your solicitor will be able to put an agreement into wording which is clear and will be accepted by the courts to in effect rubber stamp and make it into a consent order.

Your solicitor should also explain to you and cover in any financial considerations and resulting consent order:

- A 'clean break' settlement (particularly where there are no children involved)
- Point out things you might not be aware of e.g. losing out on pension rights
- Effect of any order on welfare benefit entitlements

When I first approached my solicitor she was very clear on the things I needed to speak directly with my husband about. I was terribly afraid of any conversations with my husband but she supported me and made me feel strong, she said she had every confidence in me that I could face these difficult steps head on and in so doing not rely on expensive and protracted legal processes to reach the same outcome.

After telling my solicitor my story she quite insightfully said that I had been grieving a failed marriage for quite some time and to be prepared for this grieving process to now hit my husband who had no idea I was about to leave. I found this really helpful and gave this comment a lot of thought and was able to prepare myself for some of the emotions that would come flying at me.

GROUNDS FOR DIVORCE

There is a huge amount of information on the internet about divorce - the most reliable of which can be found on good established solicitors webs sites, the information is there for free so read up and get wise.

Some Useful Links:

http://www.family-lawfirm.co.uk/divorce-and-separation/how-to-get-a-uk-divorce.aspx

http://www.lawsociety.org.uk/for-the-public/common-legal-issues/getting-a-divorce/

There is really only one ground for divorce – the irretrievable breakdown of a marriage. However when I set out on this journey I really knew very little so I have done my own summary below and hope this is helpful although I would re-emphasise the importance of consulting a solicitor. The irretrievable breakdown of a marriage is proved by establishing one or more of the following 'facts':

- **UNREASONABLE BEHAVIOUR:** It's worth bearing in mind that the court doesn't insist on really severe allegations of unreasonable behaviour in order to grant a divorce. Relatively mild allegations such as devoting too much time to a career, having no common interests or pursuing a separate social life may suffice. Using mild allegations may make it easier to agree the contents of the petition with your spouse.

- **ADULTERY**: You must prove through actual admission or through sufficient circumstantial evidence that your spouse has had sexual intercourse with another person of the opposite sex.

- **TWO YEARS' SEPARATION.**

- FIVE YEARS' SEPARATION WITHOUT CONSENT.

- DESERTION.

UNMARRIED COUPLES HAVE DIFFERENT LEGAL RIGHTS AND RESPONSIBILITIES in relation to property, finances and children to their married counterparts. Contrary to popular opinion there is no such thing as a common law husband or wife. If you are not married you will not have the same financial rights - it's important to establish what your rights are as soon as possible - this can be ascertained in your free 30 minutes with a solicitor but go prepared with as much information about your current circumstances as possible.

MEDIATION SERVICES are non-legal services that can be used to help resolve matters concerning the children and or finances. The costs are much less than using a solicitor for 100% of the negotiations and can help in reaching a mutual decision sooner and at lower cost.

BE IN CONTROL AS MUCH AS POSSIBLE if you have a case for divorcing your husband try to make sure that you protect your position during the process. The legal process can take a long time especially when you are trying to resolve the finances at the same time as gaining a divorce. So be careful with regard to your own behaviour.

You may well meet someone else during this period of time. You might have had someone else before you made the decision to leave but you don't want to jeopardize your reasons for divorce. If you are sleeping with a new partner your husband can initiate proceedings for divorce on the grounds of adultery and this may undermine your position legally; financially; socially and your own confidence levels.

WHEN IT COMES TO A NEW RELATIONSHIP it's probably sensible not to lose sight of your priorities, one of which is to extract yourself as cleanly as possible from the previous relationship so take your time, don't be put under pressure by anyone. You are your own person and can take control.

Looking back on the process you will see that six months, a year, two years is actually a short period of time so there's really no need to rush. Time is a great protector, it gives you space to think, to find yourself again, connect with the person you have wanted to be for many years.

There's a great book from **Which?** *("The Which Guide to Divorce" ISBN 1 84490 015 0) that covers everything you need to know about getting divorced – it's a bit mechanical but comprehensive.*

STEP

DOING IT FOR REAL

There are books on getting divorced; on abusive relationships and so on but none of them seem to cover the bit where you actually *tell* your partner you're leaving, so here's my attempt to fill that gap. The first consideration in communication is your children if you have them.

I'M A GREAT BELIEVER IN PROTECTING CHILDREN AS FAR AS POSSIBLE from the unpleasant details of a break up. If you're lucky enough not to have had them exposed to the rows; verbal or physical abuse and its aftermath then there's no need to involve them in any decision making about whether you should stay or leave.

CHILDREN WANT TO PROTECT BOTH PARENTS and above all want their parents to stay together; they don't want their world to fall apart. More importantly they can blame themselves for the marital breakdown – this might be more likely if they have been privy to the decision making process.

Children are the innocent parties and need your protection and your stability. I think most children can cope with a split between their parents as long as there's stability and consistency. So with this in mind - tell your partner you're leaving before you tell your children, but ideally if you can make it possible – tell your children before your partner does. Again it's about being in control. Your children need to hear the news from you - before it's twisted or loaded with additional emotion. The information you give your children needs to be clear, concise and above all black and white.

YOU CAN CHOOSE WHEN YOU TELL YOUR PARTNER YOU'RE LEAVING but it's certainly not an easy thing to do, so go easy on yourself, do it where you feel safe and comfortable. You may decide to tell him once you have left or before you go. I chose the latter option because of some strange inbred level of politeness, which I should of course have put to one side.

I had my bags packed and the girls were in the car. It was Saturday lunchtime and my husband was asleep in a chair in front of the football having eaten steak and chips and drunk a bottle of red wine.

I slipped out of the house intending to head for my mums, a two-hour drive away. But something held me back, I felt empathy for him and sadness that he would wake up and find us gone. So I told him I was going. Not surprisingly he very quickly woke up and went into panic mode. He held me against the cupboards in the kitchen and begged me to stay. After about fifteen minutes I retrieved the girls from the car. He was hysterical and it was not very nice for them to see him in that state.

I felt I had blown all my chances and spent the rest of the weekend in deep regret however on the following Monday evening I told him in a very calm and collected way that I was definitely going. There was only anger and resentment from him this time. No begging me to stay. He actually said I couldn't leave him because I was his pension. I certainly knew where I stood then.

PLAN THE BEFORE, DURING AND AFTER. Where will you be? Are you protected? Is it neutral territory. What might be the physical outcome? Will you turn and walk away or are you expecting him to. Which is easiest to pull off?

JANE: I left my husband and went to my mum's with the children after I'd picked them up from school. I asked him to come over as I needed to talk and then in the safety of my mum's house I told him I had left.

I felt secure and protected. The children were out playing with my sister's children and so were happily distracted.

My husband didn't take it very well but at that moment he had to accept it. Once he'd left I told the children what was going on. I stayed with my mum for a couple of weeks before moving into a rented house with the children.

PREPARE WHAT YOU ARE GOING TO SAY – if you're very nervous write it down and practice it. Shut your eyes and visualise saying it, visualise their reaction and how you will best deal with this reaction. Picture yourself as confident, strong and sticking to your guns.

MARIE: telling my husband was very hard. I don't think I will ever be in that situation again – seeing someone so distraught for such a long time because of what I was saying. But I had to stick to my guns and find the strength to do it. I did not want to live the life I had been living for 15 years.

DO NOT RETURN to the marital home if you have already left.

THE LANGUAGE YOU USE NEEDS TO BE ABSOLUTELY CLEAR - no grey areas, no ambiguities for them to expose and work on to weaken what you are saying.

DON'T APOLOGISE – REMEMBER IT'S NOT YOUR FAULT. Tell them you will be telling the children what has happened. Tell them you are seeking help with arrangements for the children.

If you are confident about your future arrangements, say so, for example: "You will see the children for half the week every week"', " I won't prevent the children from seeing your mother"etc.

> *Sometimes when you're nervous, words desert you. These are some you might find useful:*
>
> *- I have left you.*
>
> *- I have moved out and won't be coming back.*
>
> *- I can no longer tolerate your abusive behaviour so I have left.*
>
> *- I don't love you anymore and I am not coming back.*

TAKE THE EASIEST OPTION: Don't feel guilty about doing this. Make things as simple for yourself as they can possibly be, remember this is just one step in what will be a complicated process. If it's easier, write a note, send a text or make a phone call rather than speaking face to face. Think each of the options through and identify the one which feels the easiest and least stressful for you. Try not to empathise with your partner too much as that will only weaken your resolve.

If I had really thought about it I should have known that after a lot of initial bluster my partner was actually glad to be rid of his family responsibilities. I had too much fear of his initial reaction but in hindsight this was exaggerated in my head - he was not a very good father because he couldn't be bothered, he didn't like the responsibility. Although he initially fought to keep me this was more about saving face and hurt pride than actually wanting me to stay.

Likely responses: go through the list below and prepare what you might say or do in each of the scenarios

- *Declaration of love.*

- *Physical threat.*

- *Physical violence towards you.*

- *Verbal abuse and intimidation.*

- *Emotional blackmail.*

- *Tears and emotional breakdown.*

- *If they say "Good riddance!"*

STAYING SAFE IS VITAL, If you are even remotely concerned there may be a physical threat to you or the children then *make sure you have somewhere safe to stay.* This may be with family or you may need to contact the housing department of your local authority to see if you're eligible for temporary accommodation.

> *There are also many women's refuge centres across the UK that can be found on the internet.*
>
> *The website* **Refuge.org.uk** *provides help and advice on staying safe and contact information so that you can discuss whether there is somewhere you can stay.*

IN MY EXPERIENCE it is better to keep all communication to a minimum. This is not easy in this day and age with so many different channels of communication many of which are very personal, hard to screen and can be used against you. Social media is also out there - it's not in your control so use it very carefully. I remember Phil Collins being criticised for dumping his wife by fax – this now seems kind of quaint and old fashioned compared to dumping by Facebook, twitter or text. Try to plan all your conversations with your now ex-partner in advance. If you do meet or call them, make sure you're in the calmest frame of mind and try not to let them see how nervous you really are.

> **Find a mantra that works to give you inner strength and courage** *– try these for size:*
> - *I'm a strong woman with an independent mind.*
> - *I want to see this through and want it to be a success.*
> - *I am not afraid of my bullying ex-partner - he can no longer control me because I have left him.*
> - *We are no longer a couple. I do not have to think like a couple. I am free.*

ENSURE THE CHILDREN KNOW WHAT'S HAPPENING: it's easier to tell the children you've left rather than that you are going to leave. But as I've mentioned, don't make them part of the decision so that they won't feel they should intervene. If you're moving from the family home it's easier to tell the children if you have first removed them from the home. A child physically refusing to leave the house will present quite a big problem so try to avoid this.

> **Visualise the outcome you're trying to achieve.**
>
> *It will keep you on track and focused. Again you can utilize some of our mantras covered before:*
>
> *- I am a good mother.*
>
> *- If I don't go through with this I won't be able to be the mother I want to be.*
>
> *- I am more than strong enough to do this.*

WHAT AND HOW YOU TELL THE CHILDREN WILL DEPEND ON THEIR AGES: you'll probably want to spare them the full details behind the relationship breakdown. I would say it depends on how much they have witnessed first-hand. My own children were unaware of the rows and verbal abuse and not old enough to understand that daddy was ignoring mummy for days on end. They did however know that on many days I was very sad. Children are perceptive and protective. They don't like sad parents even if they don't know the cause.

BE ABSOLUTELY CLEAR! No frills, no wrapping things up in lots of words. Just tell it how it is . . .

- . . . "I've left daddy and we are now staying at grannies/friends/ sisters house. We're going to find a new home and we're not going back to our old house."

- . . . "Mummy and daddy are not going to be together anymore. I don't want to live with him so I have left him. You will see daddy on x days/ for half the week but mummy is not going back to live with daddy."

THERE WILL BE TEARS AND UPSET. Stay focused and on track think of your goals. Try not to feel guilty - remember this isn't your fault. You didn't ask for any of this to happen. You're removing yourself from a terrible situation to find a new you, a new life and give yourself the opportunity to be a better parent. Even if your children don't understand what you're telling them immediately they will in the coming weeks and months see you are a changed person. My children saw a new me, I had more energy, I involved the children in everyday activities; what to have for dinner; sorting washing; changing beds - overnight these activities became quite fun because I was giving them my full attention while the jobs were getting done.

We had so much family time - it was as if I'd got four more hours in the day – every day. My girls saw how happy I was and didn't question my actions. They never asked me to go back to daddy.

He of course spun a different story. He bought flowers for them to give to me, he cried endlessly in front of them and declared undying love for me. But as he only saw them every other Saturday – his influence was minimal and I stuck to my clear message. "I will never go back to daddy, I don't love him anymore."

YOUR CHILDREN ARE LIKELY TO FEEL A TORRENT OF MIXED EMOTIONS if there are any of these which you feel unable to deal with, don't be afraid to look outside for help and support, ask your supportive friend/ sister how they would handle it. Below are a few of the reactions/emotions your children may experience:

- **ANGER**: this can be a good emotion, it's often short term and allowing it to come out is good so don't be afraid of it. Let it come out then perhaps encourage them to go outside for some fresh air and a calm down.

- **SADNESS**: A very natural reaction. Acknowledge that it is natural, perhaps counteract by explaining how life is now going to be different but better. Comfort and take comfort, make it a two way thing.

- **BLAME**: an angry child will look quickly to blame you and immediate blame can be as swift and as vicious as a bout of food poisoning. Try not to be too defensive or too hurt. A longer term build-up of blame can be more problematic. If your partner is manipulating the children using them to undermine your new life - blame for what's happened will inevitably be laid on you. Hold your head up high. The situation was not of your making, you didn't choose to be in an abusive relationship. Keep your behaviour balanced, don't retaliate or lower yourself to your partner's level. Keep your dignity and kindness and eventually your children will see the truth. (although it may take time).

- **SELF-BLAME**: many children will blame themselves for what has happened. They feel involved and they are, after all, a pivotal part of the family unit. You therefore have to be supremely cautious about what you say and how it's said. I once overheard a mother on the phone telling her 5 year old "Please behave when mummy's not there, you know how cross daddy gets with mummy when you're a naughty boy." Putting that responsibility on a child makes no sense and of course leads to self-blame. A child who's blaming themselves needs reassurance – constantly. They also need to lighten up – the new life is about having fun so make sure the children are given plenty of it. It doesn't have to cost money. My neighbor amazed me by building a pond no bigger than a postage stamp in her back yard. She used some old bricks she found beneath a hedge, a plastic fertilizer bag and some rocks. A few goldfish and she and her three children had themselves a pond, a new hobby and lots of fun.

- **INTROSPECTION:** it's very hard when your children won't open up. You can talk as much as you like but if they won't respond, it can become really tough.

My younger daughter used to wake up bright and happy but about twenty minutes after waking it was as if a dark cloud descended and I couldn't get through. It was very sad. Every day was the same, such promise and then such sadness.

I was lucky, her school suggested counseling through 'art therapy'. After 8 weeks of the therapy we had a review meeting. The counselors talked about her learning difficulties and how I possibly was not relaxed enough about that. Perhaps I was fighting it and hoping it would go away. They suggested I accept the problem and discuss it openly at home. The fact that I currently didn't was putting my daughter under a huge amount of pressure. So Jo's difficulties became an open subject. Something we discussed over meal times. It was miraculous - the dark clouds started to clear and I had my sunny daughter shining through again.

- **RELIEF:** you may not have been aware of just how much your children knew about what was going on between you and your partner. They may have been very scared for you and the move from the family home may come as a huge relief, achieving what they thought was impossible.

- **DELIGHT:** again if they feel relieved they may also be extremely happy. Make sure you allow this happiness to pour out. Don't be shocked by it – welcome it as a sign of things to come.

- **GRIEF:** grief goes very deep, it's more than sadness, it's a long process and one that needs patience and understanding. Don't look for a quick fix or believe you should be able to make the grief go away. Often grief is not because of actual events but a mourning for something that might have been for example, a better relationship with your father, the relationship you wish your parents had had and now never will. There are some great homeopathic remedies for helping with grief and if you know someone who practices homeopathy it's well worth asking their advice.

- **FEAR:** fear is real. After all that's the basis of the abuse. Your partner has played on your fear. So your child having their own fears is not surprising. You'll need to be reassuring and acknowledge that fear, don't brush it under the carpet. Fear can lead to sleepless nights, bed-wetting, and uncharacteristic behaviour. All these things need to be seen in the current context and are normal and to be expected. Patience, understanding and reassurance are what's needed by the bucket load.

BE PREPARED FOR FAMILY AND FRIENDS TO BE SHOCKED AND GRIEF STRICKEN. It's likely that you have kept you unhappiness hidden from them and they will be sure initially that you're going through a phase and that things can be patched up and carry on as they were. People generally don't like change and will not want you to disrupt their neat life. Be ready for this and remind yourself that it is your life and only you knew what it was really like to be that unhappy. Make sure that when you tell a wider audience your plans are quite firm so you can feel confident in standing your ground. You're not asking their advice you are telling them that you have left.

THE ACTUAL MOVE

When I knew for sure that I was going and the actual date, I prepared the house – I went through each cupboard and rearranged it so that the things I wanted to take were all in one place. I didn't want to take much. Nothing of any value meant anything to me anymore. When it came to the day of the move I went around just putting the prearrange items into boxes – the whole thing took no more than an hour.

Before moving into my rented house I drew up a list of the essential things I needed and was lucky enough to find several of my friends had items to spare which were on my list. I hired a van and did a little tour collecting all the furniture that I needed.

I then hit Wilko, the best shop for a distressed woman, I went to the check out with a trolly full of everything you can imagine – tin opener, knives and forks, tea towels, pegs, iron, washing up bowel etc. the woman at the check out said "Blimey, you setting up home?" To which I replied proudly "Yes, yes I am!"

YOU MIGHT HAVE TO LEAVE THINGS OF VALUE BEHIND. I left the dinner service, the cutlery set, all ornaments and knick nacks. I didn't take any framed photos but I did take photo albums. When I left the house you couldn't really tell I had removed anything. This meant my husband had very little to throw at me in terms of what I had removed - although he did ask for the lemon squeezer back!

YOU MIGHT NEED TO BORROW A CAR OR A VAN. One or two trips might be necessary and you may need to plan the whole thing around when your partner is definitely not going to be in. It will be easier and less distressing for all concerned if they are not there. It's certainly not a good idea to do the move with the children. Seeing items moved out of somewhere they have viewed as the family home will be upsetting and unsettling and make for a bad start to some difficult times ahead.

HAVING MOVED everything into your new place *make the beds* before you introduce the children to their new home, there's nothing worse to a child than a bare mattress. Put on their favorite duvets or buy some fun covers from Asda or Wilko's, little distractions like this will take some of the pressure off you.

PLAN THE MEAL so you have all the food in and then introduce the children to their new home. They will need to see you looking confident and strong, wavering over dinner and then going out to do the food shop will undermine this position. You need to make things as easy for you and the children as possible and immediately after the move you almost need to hibernate – you don't need contact with the outside world on the first night. Just be at home with the children and provide them with endless amounts of attention which in itself will be a comfort.

Marie: People were so kind, I had so many things given to me to help set up a new home that I didn't need to buy any furniture. It meant I could afford the move. I'd saved up the deposit for the rented house but if I hadn't been able to afford it I would have asked my mum or my sister.

SOURCES OF SUPPORT

As well as a close confidant you might also need a network of other people who can help you and it's probably a good idea to think this through beforehand.

TRANSPORT may be an issue if you don't have a car. So look around to see who might help you getting the children to school. In exchange for any favour received you can always offer reciprocal help perhaps baby-sitting, so there's exchange rather than obligation.

CHILDREN NEED AN OUTLET and play dates with friends can be a great release and source of normality – you can set this up in advance. You might also get additional support from school as long as you communicate and tell them what's going on

TELL THEM AT WORK WHAT'S GOING ON. Even if you don't give them the full details, if you manage expectations most employers will be understanding and supportive.

LOCAL GROUPS CAN BE A GOD-SEND and it's easier than ever these days to find out what's going on in your area for single parents or families needing a little extra help. Research in advance what's going on in your area and where you may be able to go for some moral support, back-to-work training, or parent counseling and advice.

YOU MAY LOSE FRIENDS in the move away from your partner, I certainly did. I expected our mutual friends to not do the 'journey' with me and this turned out to be the case. I lost loads of 'friends' – a little like you might lose a cardigan, they fell off along the wayside as I went through the move. These were obviously not the closest of friends but you do need to be prepared. One of the advantages of sharing the childcare with you ex husband is that you will hopefully find that you often have free time on a Saturday - which is great for meeting up with friends in similar circumstances as your own and gives you opportunity for some child free time – going for lunch a shopping trip or to the football. It's the silver lining.

STEP
YOUR NEW LIFE

3

This is it - you've made it through the door into a world of freedom. It's taken an enormous amount of strength to get here so first of all congratulate yourself. Well done!

IT'S REALLY IMPORTANT to guard your new-found freedom very carefully, it has taken a lot of effort, money and emotional upheaval to get to this position so be wary of giving it up again all too easily, just because you're not used to it. Sometimes if you have a sick animal and have to keep them in a cage, once they have recovered the animal continues to sleep in the cage because they've got used to it and it feels comforting - don't let that be you!

THIS IS YOUR CHANCE TO BE YOU, your true self. It will take time to find yourself again so don't give up when faced with the first hurdle. You're strong (never forget, you've been strong enough to get to this point) and you will be OK. You have made the right decision, so carry on being brave a while longer. Your confidence will return; your energy levels will soar. You will find each day exciting, the opportunity for adventure. So don't go wasting it!

FEELING HAPPY IS ESSENTIAL. It helps us keep healthy and care for loved ones. We've already established that without an underlying happiness it is difficult to function. However it can be difficult to identify the little things that are making our mood dip.

THINK CAREFULLY ABOUT what puts you into a 'bad mood'. What upsets you or plays on your mind making you feel anxious; feeds an inner self doubt and makes you slump into a mini depression? And more importantly can you change your mood? Are you in control of how you feel? *Yes - yes you are!* In fact you're the only person you really do have control over.

So pay attention to how you're feeling and learn some exercises that work for you to help shift your mood and energy levels. Here are just a few ideas:

> - **Smile;** *just putting a smile on your face when you feel yourself slumping can reverse the downward trend of the day.*
> - **Say hello;** *be attentive to people close to you, give them your time and attention. Be compassionate and caring.*
> - **Stop your inner critic;** *at the end of each day think about the good things that have happened; congratulate yourself on something that made you happy.*
> - **Exercise;** *even going for a walk round the block can shift your energy and avoid dipping into a depressive mood.*
> - **Appreciate;** *everything around you; children; food; fabrics; nature and being single!*

SPENDING QUALITY TIME WITH YOUR CHILDREN CAN ENHANCE YOUR MOOD and dancing round the kitchen to a favorite family record never fails to boost everyone's sense of wellbeing. You don't need to spoil or over-indulge them. Reassure yourself, remember you had to leave and it wasn't your fault so there's no need to feel guilty. Feeling guilty is a negative emotion which leaves you vulnerable to over-indulging the kids. It also leaves you vulnerable to them manipulating the situation - as we know, children will want things back just how they were so they may show a complete disregard for your wellbeing! But it's really your time they will need so go for a picnic in the park; grab a take away pizza and a good DVD; go for a walk or visit a local attraction.

MONEY CAN BE A CAUSE OF GREAT ANXIETY. So try to be in control as much as possible and don't stick your head in the sand. It can be daunting at first to consider every element of your finances but once you have the basics covered you may find it empowering and confidence boosting to have a handle on your finances. The budget below covers most aspects of day to day living,

DO AN INITIAL ASSESSMENT OF WHAT YOU NEED IN YOUR BUDGET and if you find your expenditure exceeds your income, scrutinize the list below and identify what can be eliminated. For example is taking the children to the hairdressers essential or might you have a friend who's a dab hand with the scissors?

LEAVE ROOM FOR THE UNEXPECTED: You may suddenly find your car needs new tyres or your boiler has expired. Identify what may come up unexpectedly and set up a slush fund into which you pay a monthly set amount for emergencies.

KEEP A PIGGY BANK IN THE KITCHEN and reward the children by popping a couple of pound coins in every now and again. When the piggy's full it will pay for a family treat.

	Monthly	Annually	Essential?
ACCOMMODATION			
mortgage/rent			
council tax			
water rates			
electricity			
gas			
oil/solid fuel			
broadband			
phone			
ground rent			
SUB TOTAL			
HOUSEHOLD EXPENSES			
food			
house insurance			
contents insurance			
repairs			
tv licence			
cleaner			
window cleaner			
SUB TOTAL			

CAR

Insurance			
tax			
petrol			
loan			
SUB TOTAL			

CHILDREN

school uniform			
shoes/trainers			
outings			
clubs			
nappies			
dentist			
hairdresser			
childminder			
books			
toys			
presents			
SUB TOTAL			

	Monthly	Annually	Essential?
PERSONAL EXPENSES			
hairdressers			
beauticians			
dentist			
prescriptions			
Opticians			
dry cleaning			
travel to work			
travel for leisure			
lunch at work			
holidays			
legal fees			
SUB TOTAL			

GRAND TOTAL _____

HAPPY BEING SINGLE

It's far better to be single than with the wrong partner, however there is a lot of prejudice in our society towards single people.

I remember my father saying that any available man my age (I was 35) would either be a mummy's boy or be mentally unstable – no stereo typing there then!

MARRIED WOMEN MAY GIVE YOU THE COLD SHOULDER, suddenly you are seen as a threat and highly likely to run off with their husbands. Remind yourself that this is their insecurity not yours and find yourself some more stoic and supportive friends. It never ceases to amaze me how horrible people can be – so be prepared take a deep breath and brace yourself for some very odd acts of prejudice. Trust me you will be able to laugh about them in the future.

I moved from Leeds to the outskirts of London six months into my new found singledom. I was amazed at the prejudice there was towards me. On one occasion whilst having my daughter assessed by a GP as part of my application for her special needs statement, the GP said one of my daughter's problems at school was due to us being a different social class to everyone else. I asked her what she meant and her reply was "well you're a single parent" I was shocked and horrified and sadly, only afterwards thought of the many different responses I could and should have made.

BUT DON'T WORRY THERE ARE SOME GREAT BENEFITS OF BEING SINGLE.

- You can make all the decisions without a continuous opposing, critical voice. It's you who can decide what to have for dinner; what to do at the weekend; whether the kids should attend afterschool club; whether you go round to your mum's for tea; what time to put the children to bed - the list is endless and your new-found decision-making freedom will feel like a breath of fresh air.

- Suddenly your mind is clearer, you're free to think– and the main thing you'll find yourself saying is, "What's the worst that can happen? If I screw it up it will only be me to reproach myself."

- I discovered "To Me From Me" a great excuse for treats – I bought myself some great Christmas presents – real treats and of course nothing I really needed. Make the most of your time to indulge yourself because some of the best treats can be free: it may be a nice solitary walk, time with friends, back to back episodes of Sex and the City; a soak in the bath or just sitting down with a good book. Make sure you give yourself the time to really appreciate this new found freedom

AVOID THE THINGS THAT LEAD TO THAT HOLLOW LONELY FEELING. For me it was things like the school fete and holidays with the children. In one confident moment I booked a holiday to Portugal but it was a mistake as I felt very lonely surrounded by happy families. I found the whole thing draining and decided to holiday with family thereafter. So it was repeated camping trips to Devon and Wales and we have some fabulous memories of this time. Don't feel you need to compete on the holiday front with your ex, just do what is natural, comfortable and least daunting for you.

ON THE OTHER HAND I HAD SOME GREAT HOLIDAYS AS A SINGLE GAL. I booked onto holidays where it was likely most people would be single – sports holidays, that sort of thing. They were a great confidence boost and a brilliant break from being mum 24 hours a day.

SET NEW PATTERNS. You may want to make some radical changes to the way you've done things in the past. For example you may have always gone to your mother's for Christmas but this year you might not have your children with you and a big family Christmas with other people's children albeit nieces and nephews may not be an encouraging prospect.

So you have full permission to do things differently. If you don't want to socialize at Christmas then don't. Go on holiday instead or spend Christmas with a friend who doesn't have children. Break the patterns and do things differently. It will make you feel in control and bold!

KEEP A JOURNAL. I'm not great at looking backwards, I prefer to think of what's ahead. However, sometimes just making a note of the good things that have happened in a day can be held on to and provide an anchor on bad days.

In one of many recent hormonal sleepless nights when I was worrying about everyone and everything I got up and wrote a list headed Good Things. Big things, little things, I wrote down everything I could think of which came under the heading and had happened that day, week, month, year. It made me feel a whole lot better, back in control and I was able to go back to sleep.

NEW RELATIONSHIPS

Don't be in a hurry when it comes to a new relationship. The priority is to extract yourself as cleanly as possible from the previous one, so take your time, don't be put under pressure by anyone. You are your own person and can take control. Looking back you'll see that six months, a year, two years is actually not a long time and there's really no need to rush. Time is a great protector, it gives you space to think, to find yourself again and connect with the person you may have wanted to be for many years.

YOUR CONFIDENCE IN A RELATIONSHIP WILL HAVE TAKEN A BATTERING and you need to give yourself time to re-establish yourself before getting heavily involved in a new relationship. If you don't do this, you run the risk of making the same mistakes again. Be sure of the qualities you value and have the confidence to stick to them.

IT'S FRIGHTENINGLY EASY TO FALL FOR THE FIRST MAN WHO APPEARS GENTLE AND KIND after what you've been through and it has to be said there are people out there who actively look for those in a vulnerable position. Your need of their attention is an ego boost for them. So be careful. Know your values and hold onto them. Keep your life simple and don't jeopardise the hard-won independence you've gained from leaving your partner.

IF IT ISN'T NECESSARY FOR YOUR NEW PARTNER TO MEET YOUR EX THEN KEEP IT THAT WAY, it's simpler!

HOWEVER IF YOU HAVE CHILDREN or still live near your ex, you need to consider and pre-empt that meeting. You will be trying to continue a civilized relationship with your ex because of the children. Your new partner needs to understand and respect this and not mistake it for affection or regret. On the other hand there's no doubt it can be so hard to maintain a relationship with your ex when you may still be resentful or angry but unable to express this because of the children. You need your new partner to respect all of your feelings and fully support you.

IF YOU ARE LOOKING FOR A NEW PARTNER then my advice is to do a lot of the things you like to do and you will hopefully find a like-minded individual along the way. My mum found her new partner in her local ramblers group; my dad's partner is a fellow bell-ringer. A friend of mine met her new man at a local dog show another through a local cycling group. I met my new husband at work when I moved to London. My view is that this sort of initial meeting is more natural than the internet and not half as harsh!

YOU WILL HAVE GOOD DATES, BAD DATES AND TERRIBLE DATES, as long as you don't dwell on the worst bits as they are all par for the course.

IF YOUR PLANS INCLUDE INTERNET DATING then this should be looked at as a numbers game. Everyone who is using the internet is talking to or dating a lot of people - it's a bit like going for a job interview. Don't fall for people online! A meeting is essential. But try not to take it too seriously in the early stages. Don't take the rejection personally and if you can't stand the heat then 'stay out of the kitchen!' as you will find the whole business confidence destroying.

REGAINING YOUR CONFIDENCE

Attention from the opposite sex will always be a boost to confidence and is nice to receive but there other ways to rebuild self-esteem:

- **SET YOURSELF** a personal physical challenge, exercise doesn't have to cost – a ten mile walk may be a good first goal, a five k run or a mile swim. List what appeals and when you cross it off the list, that's a great feeling. It's very easy to put off that first run - so tell yourself you're going out for just ten minutes. If you feel you want to go on further - you have your trainers on so run!

- **JOIN** a local exercise club – dancing, running, cycling – again none of these have to be expensive.

- **MAKE THE BEST OF YOURSELF** at all times. Take a good look in the mirror -how are your clothes, hair, make-up? Could you do with a bit of an overhaul? Ask your friends to help – a shopping trip or assistance with a new style of make-up. When you know you're looking your best your confidence will increase.

- **SET YOURSELF AN INTELLECTUAL CHALLENGE.** You may not have had time to read much over the past few years – list some books you want to read, or join a book club. Second hand bookshops are in abundance so again, this doesn't have to cost very much. Escaping with a good book is a great way to refresh your mind.

- Take up a new hobby or study something that grabs your interest such as a new language or baking bread! In fact kneading can be a great stress buster and something the children love to do too.

About six months after leaving my husband I drew up a calendar – it showed how often I would go running, out with friends or do something special with my children. It listed what things were to be completed - such as having my teeth cleaned; my hair highlighted; buying a new pair of boots:

I gave myself points for targets achieved and totted them up at the end of the month. I'm mad on lists so even just the writing of them and the crossing off gave me satisfaction. I found Christmas and winter generally quite hard to deal with so a calendar of events and a chart of things to do helped the cold days whizz by.

I identified friends in a similar position to me and spent quite a bit of time with them for moral support – we went on family outings together and met for lunch when it was just the two of us on Saturdays. We would help each other through the good and bad times.

AN ABUSIVE RELATIONSHIP may deflate sexual desires completely. It may have left you feeling that 'sexy' is somehow wrong. Your husband may have accused you of being tarty or provocative. Your thoughts about your own sexuality are possibly completely muddled. So you need to get back to basics and find your sexiness again.

MY ADVICE IS CHILL OUT AND LIGHTEN UP. You'll make mistakes, everyone does they just don't talk about them very often. But life is full of ups and downs and finding yourself in bed with the most unsuitable of partners is one of these little hillocks.

AS LONG AS YOUR CHILDREN ARE NOT AFFECTED by your mistakes then you only have yourself to worry about. You do though need to protect the children. Avoid relationships with anyone connected to their school for example and don't introduce them to all of your dates – again there's no rush – you need to be absolutely sure of your new partner before introducing them to the children and in my view this can take about six months.

SEX CAN BE THE FIRST STEPS to finding a new inner confidence, but as we all know, you don't really need a new partner to rediscover your inner sex goddess. Feeling sexy isn't based on how you look on the outside - you need to feel right on the inside too and a great way to start connecting with your body again is Pilates. These simple exercises work on the inner muscles around your pelvic floor. You can do the exercises at any time – while waiting for a bus or reading a book but done regularly you will start to feel more engaged with that part of your body. Remember, the perfect body doesn't exist for any woman, so simply focus on your best features and make the most of them. And make the most of your new-found privacy. Have fun - go to bed early and explore!

A SHOULDER TO CRY ON is helpful and there are a lot of professional shoulders (coaches, counselors) around if you have the budget and prefer to pay for an 'outside ear'. If this isn't your choice or budget doesn't allow, look at all your friends and contacts, who do you look up to and admire? Would they be willing to provide some advice maybe in a specific direction such as career or parenting?

IN LOOKING FOR A 'MENTOR' you are choosing someone who is not in competition with you. It's amazing how many relationships are tainted by competition. It may be a sibling where one can't bear to be outdone by the other or a best friend who has always perceived you as an underdog. When things change the friend might not like the shift in power balance.

HEALTH AND WELLBEING

Ok so this is the new you! A new world with you right in the middle and number one. Yes the children are always going to be your priority but it's time to start focusing on your own health and wellbeing. If you're healthy this goes a long way to making you happy and if you're happy the children are happy too: healthy body healthy mind, healthy family!

FITNESS. You don't have to be an athlete, but a form of exercise about 3 times a week will have a dramatic effect on your fitness levels. If you struggle to go upstairs without panting and puffing at the top – it's time to get your trainers on and go for a 30 minute fast pace walk. There are many urban walking groups that would provide company and the motivation.

DIET. Nutrition is crucial for you and the children. Sometimes we can feel our eating patterns are out of control – if this is the case just bring everything back to basics remembering it's all about balance. We need to eat a little of everything but in the right amounts. It's no good just eating protein or carbs or starving yourself for a week and eating nothing but cabbage as this is not sustainable nor is it a good model for the children.

The more food you can prepare from scratch the more control you have over what you eat.

Magazines are a good source of healthy balanced recipes – often providing a weekly programme of family meals. They usually provide nutritional information as well so you can check on your calorie intake too if this is important to you.

CONSIDER ALTERNATIVE THERAPIES that can support you through what will undoubtedly be a stressful period (although in my experience not as stressful as living with emotional abuse!). Take a look into what Homeopathy, reflexology and even hypnosis have to offer in terms of helping you with mental pressures and mixed emotions such as grief and anger.

WOBBLES!

Leaving an abuser is a bit like having your tonsils out. When I had my tonsils out at age 35, everyone told me how painful and uncomfortable it would be. The surgeon afterwards said I was remarkably cheerful given how much pain I must be in. I said that he could never have experienced really bad tonsillitis. A tonsillectomy was nothing! So the pain after leaving a bully is often nowhere near what you've already been through.

BUT THERE WILL BE BAD DAYS when you fall into a deep well of self-pity and despair. For me these days are aligned with PMT. If you see a pattern based on your cycle, try and pre-empt it. Keep track of the dates and take care of yourself at times when you know you're going to be vulnerable. Try to be around family and friends who can take some of the pressure off. And if all else fails, go to bed early and hope tomorrow is a better day!

> **I found poetry** *particularly comforting there are some great anthologies by* **Daisy Goodwin** *that I used to read in the middle of the night. The poems were full of empathy and humour.*

COLD DARK NIGHTS can sometimes seem very long when you're on your own – don't be afraid of not sleeping. Make a cup of tea, turn on the lights, grab a good book and above all relax. No one ever died from insomnia and the more you fight it the less you'll sleep.

DON'T GO BACKWARDS! AND DON'T GO BACK! It's really important that your bad days don't eat into your resilience. Your partner may be on bended knee to persuade you to go back. Be strong remember how difficult it was to leave and how wonderful it is to be free. If you go back all this will be gone, you will once again lose all your power, and probably be in a weaker position than you were to start with.

IF YOU HAVE CHILDREN your partner may try to manipulate them if you return to the family home; turning them against you so that if you attempt to leave again they may refuse to come with you.

YOUR PARTNER WAS A BULLY and will still be a bully so don't give into any persuasive talk. He may feel insulted because you left, his pride is damaged and more importantly he has lost his power over you. If you return, all this will be fixed for him but not you. So be strong. Your partner will stop nagging if you stay consistent.

> *Close down all conversations; refuse to meet him and keep going back with the same message:*
> *- I shall not be returning. I have left you and don't love you anymore.*
> *- I am not coming back - ever*

MARIE: I had a major wobble when my ex had a new partner who didn't seem to like the children, I couldn't bear the thought of them being in the house with her and her not giving them the attention they needed. She also seemed to be very threatened by me. It made me miss the family unit I used to have and filled me with self-doubt. I soon got over that when I saw my ex inebriated as usual when I came to collect the kids from his house.

ZERO TOLERANCE FOR BAD BEHAVIOUR FROM NOW ON! Remember you don't need to put up with that any more -it's why you've left but you will have become so accustomed to it in the past that you might be forgiven for thinking it will be part of the future. It shouldn't. So, don't ever stand for it. *You are now your own person and can have you own boundaries.*

TO SUM UP. As I said right at the start - this book is not meant to be a marriage breaker but if you're caught in the trap of a deeply unhappy and unhealthy relationship, I hope that it will in fact give you the courage and the permission to leave and find a new start.

My generation was very much taught that 'Once you make your bed you have to lie in it', but this is an untruth and you need to ignore nagging old sayings like this. It's your life, your only life and you need to live it to the full and this means being happy.

Review your current situation for what it is in the cold light of day – preferably when you're not on an emotional high or low as described before but when you're feeling stable and level headed. Write a few notes on how you would like things to be, what the future could hold for you. Then write down the steps you need to take to make this happen.

Refer to the chapters above over and over because this should make the next steps more do-able and increase your confidence.

The chapters have hopefully enforced the fact that there is nothing stopping you leaving your destructive relationship. Lack of money shouldn't be an obstacle; what friends and family might think shouldn't be an obstacle and the fear of being single again shouldn't be an obstacle.

EVERY DAY CAN BRING A MINI CELEBRATION. I hope your new life brings you great happiness as it did me. I was high on fresh air from the day I left and still am. I have time to appreciate everything around me, from the smell of an autumn morning to a laugh during a family mealtime. I don't feel harassed or permanently scared. I don't feel angry and resentful all the time. I feel real and I am extremely grateful for having been able to change my life. I hope that this book helps you to find the confidence to do it too.

* * *

Further Reading

When Love Goes Wrong: Ann Jones & Susan Schechter
ISBN 0060923695

The Verbally Abusive Relationship: Patricia Evans
ISBN 1440504636

The Emotionally Abusive Relationship: Beverley Engel
ISBN 0471454038

Power and Control,
Why Charming Men Make Dangerous Lovers: Sandra Horley
ISBN 0091884322

Living with the Dominator: Pat Craven
ISBN 0955882702

The Which Guide to Divorce:
ISBN 184490 015 0

Why does he do that?: Lundy Bancroft
ISBN: 0425191656

Thank You!

I would like to thank my daughters for being so understanding and supportive about this book, and also for being incredible supporters over the last 12 years. We've had our ups and downs but stuck together throughout. Your trust in me has never faltered and I thank you for that. You are confident, gorgeous girls and I hope your strong inner confidence helps you to avoid the mistakes I made.

I would like to thank Eddie, my lovely husband for his unending support and enthusiasm.

Thank you to my wonderful family for their support even when they didn't know the full story.

Thank you to Sylvia Baldock of the Athena Network, without your workshops the book wouldn't have got beyond the pages on my computer. Thank you to my fellow 'dynorods', you are all fab. Thank you to Laurenne Dorgan for the beautiful cover design.

And last but not least thank you to Marilyn Messik, my editor, confidante and mentor. We've had lots of fun on the way.

Biography

Born in 1967 in Shropshire Katie is a mother of three. Caroline (21) and Jo (18) by her first marriage and Tom (6) by her second marriage.

Katie studied clothing and textiles at Leeds Polytechnic before pursuing a career in advertising. She moved into the energy industry in 1995 and currently runs her own successful energy consultancy of seven years with her husband Eddie.

She lives in Buckinghamshire and is a regular boater on the Thames being the proud owner of a 1920's river cruiser. Together with her husband and a few friends (and yes she often questions her sanity!) she's a bit of an exercise addict and has tackled Olympic Triathlons, one being at Hever Castle, in aid of charity and she hopes to do many more in the future.

When not launching herself into extreme physical activity, Katie has a passion for playing the flute, walking in deepest darkest Shropshire and making huge quantities of marmalade.